DATE DUE

Searchlight
BOOKS™

Animal
Superpowers

Frozen
Frogs

and Other Amazing
Hibernators

Mary Lindeen

Lerner Publications ◆ Minneapolis

 For Benjamin and Jeremy

Lerner Publications Company
A division of Lerner Publishing Group, Inc.
241 First Avenue North
Minneapolis, MN 55401 USA

For reading levels and more information, look up this title
at www.lernerbooks.com.

Library of Congress Cataloging-in-Publication Data

Names: Lindeen, Mary, author.
Title: Frozen frogs and other amazing hibernators / by Mary Lindeen.
Description: Minneapolis : Lerner Publications, 2016. | Includes bibliographical references
    and index. | Audience: Ages 8–11. | Audience: Grades 4–6.
Identifiers: LCCN 2016018630 (print) | LCCN 2016029824 (ebook) |
    ISBN 9781512425475 (lb : alk. paper) | ISBN 9781512431131 (pb : alk. paper) |
    ISBN 9781512428209 (eb pdf)
Subjects: LCSH: Hibernation—Juvenile literature.
Classification: LCC QL755 .L56 2016 (print) | LCC QL755 (ebook) |
    DDC 591.56/5—dc23

LC record available at https://lccn.loc.gov/2016018630

Manufactured in the United States of America
1-41315-23259-5/27/2016

Contents

Chapter 1

FROZEN FROGS

Animals in warm habitats have to protect themselves from heat. Animals in cooler habitats have to protect themselves from cold. Some animals that live in places with cold winters grow more fur. But sometimes animals simply sleep through the winter and wake up when it is easier to survive. These animals are hibernators.

Hibernators often sleep in dens or other hidden spots. What is a hibernator?

Wood frogs are hibernators. They live in forests as far north as the Arctic Circle. When the weather is warm, they live under logs or in wetlands. When it gets cold, they burrow under fallen leaves on the forest floor. Then they freeze solid for the whole winter!

Wood frogs are the only frogs that live north of the Arctic Circle.

Frogsicles

Most animals die if they freeze. The sharp edges of ice crystals in frozen blood can harm their bodies. But wood frogs are different. Freezing actually allows them to survive in cold weather!

A frozen wood frog does not move. It doesn't breathe. Its heart doesn't beat. Its blood doesn't flow. Ice surrounds its internal organs. Ice crystals form between its skin and muscles. About two-thirds of the water in its body freezes. But none of this kills a wood frog.

When a wood frog freezes, its eyes turn white because the lenses freeze.

Compare It!

Arctic ground squirrels can also survive in extremely cold temperatures. They hibernate in burrows for seven to eight months each winter. During that time, their body temperature drops below freezing. Hibernating arctic ground squirrels have the lowest body temperature ever recorded for any mammal. Sleeping ground squirrels warm themselves up every two to three weeks by shivering and shaking for several hours at a time. Then they stop shaking, and their bodies cool off again.

An arctic ground squirrel breathes only about three times a minute when it hibernates. Its heart beats one or two times per minute.

Amphibians with Antifreeze

Wood frogs survive because they have a secret weapon: sugar. A wood frog makes a kind of sugary syrup in its liver. This special sugar gets into the frog's blood. The sugar keeps some of the water in the frog's cells from turning to ice. It protects the cells from completely drying up and killing the frog.

The sugar in a frog's blood that helps it survive is called glucose. Humans have glucose in their bodies too!

Spring into Action

Wood frogs thaw out in the spring. The frog's heart begins to beat first. Then its brain begins to work again. And then it can move its legs and hop away into the forest. Wood frog eggs can also freeze and thaw without harm. The eggs stop developing in winter. They finish developing and then hatch when the weather warms up. Those must be some tough tadpoles!

WOOD FROG EGGS CAN SURVIVE IN TEMPERATURES BELOW FREEZING.

Chapter 2

LOW-ENERGY LEMURS

Human beings, apes, and monkeys all belong to the group of animals known as primates. So do fat-tailed dwarf lemurs. This type of lemur is the only member of the primate group known to hibernate. These small nocturnal primates live in Madagascar, a tropical island off the coast of Africa.

Some parts of the world don't have cold winters. Why might an animal hibernate if it lives where the weather is warm all year long?

Animals usually hibernate when it is the most difficult to find food. The same is true for fat-tailed dwarf lemurs. They hibernate for up to seven months during the dry season. That's when there are fewer things for them to eat. The lemurs eat a lot of food during the rainy season. Fat-tailed dwarf lemurs gain a lot of weight during this time. They store the extra fat in their tails.

Fat-tailed dwarf lemurs eat fruit, flowers, and insects.

Compare It!

Bears are among the most well-known hibernators. Just like fat-tailed lemurs, some bears eat a lot of food and gain a lot of weight before their winter sleep. Bears don't eat during hibernation. They live off of their stored fat while in their dens. But some scientists are not sure that bears actually hibernate. They do not show the same behaviors as most true animal hibernators. Other scientists think that bears hibernate but in a different way than other animals.

Bears "recycle" their urine as they sleep. Their bodies can reuse some of the nutrients contained in their waste.

Fueled by Fat

Stored fat comes in handy during hibernation. Fat-tailed dwarf lemurs need to live off their stored fat when they hibernate. The lemurs don't use as much energy during hibernation because they are not active. Their breathing becomes much slower. Their heart rate does too. This helps the fat they've stored in their bodies last longer.

A LEMUR'S TAIL GETS VERY BIG DURING THE WET MONTHS BECAUSE OF ALL THE FAT STORED THERE.

Fat-tailed dwarf lemurs hibernate in holes in trees. Their body temperature seems to match the temperature of the air around them during this time. A fat-tailed dwarf lemur's temperature is usually around 98°F (37°C). But when it hibernates, the lemur can have a body temperature as low as 41°F (5°C).

It would be a waste of energy for a lemur to try to keep its body warm.

Sleepy Little Lemurs

Scientists have discovered that hibernating lemurs do not go into deep sleep. Most animals, including humans, need some periods of deep sleep to survive. Sleep restores the energy an animal needs to stay alive. Fat-tailed dwarf lemurs appear to stay in a state of light sleep when they hibernate. This means they can survive for months without deep sleep. Scientists think this might be possible because the lemurs use so little energy when they hibernate. These little primates are big energy savers.

Most animals will die if they do not have deep sleep. But the little lemur survives for months during hibernation without deep sleep!

Chapter 3

SLUMBERING SNAILS

A snail carries its home on its back. But when the weather gets cold, a snail can't just turn up the heat to stay warm. That's a problem for a snail. A snail's body is made of mostly water. The water in its body will freeze into ice crystals if the snail gets too cold. This could kill the snail. But snails have a way of surviving in cold temperatures. They hibernate.

A snail can't survive a cold winter. Where can a snail go to survive during the winter?

Where to Go in Winter

Snails first need to find a good place to wait out the cold weather. They look for small, safe places that will protect them from frost. Snails in the woods might tuck themselves into a pile of leaves, in old logs, or under rocks. Garden snails might spend the winter in a crack in the sidewalk, next to the toolshed, or under a flowerpot. Sometimes a group of snails will settle in together.

ONLY SNAILS THAT LIVE WHERE IT GETS COLD NEED TO HIBERNATE.

Marvelous Mucus

Finding the right spot to hibernate is an important part of snail survival. So is mucus. Snails make mucus to help them move. A snail moves by stretching and sliding its foot across the ground. A snail's body is soft. The ground can be rough. Mucus helps a snail slide across the ground more safely and easily.

Snails have a foot! A snail's foot stretches from behind the snail's head to the end of its tail.

A snail also needs mucus when it hibernates. A snail uses mucus to seal off the opening of its shell so it will not dry out during hibernation. A snail uses its body to mix this sticky mucus with pieces of leaves, bits of rock, and dirt. Then it pulls its body up into its shell. It uses the foot end of its body to spread the mucus mixture across the opening of its shell. Then the mucus dries. The snail is safely sealed in its shell.

A SNAIL'S PROTECTIVE LAYER OF DRY MUCUS AND DIRT IS CALLED AN EPIPHRAGM.

Snowed In

A snail might make several of these mucus doors during hibernation. Sometimes snails will come out of their shells on mild days. Then they have to reseal themselves in their shells if the weather gets colder again. Snails will also curl up more tightly in their shell as the weather gets colder. Sometimes they'll make a second or third mucus seal farther up in the shell to keep warm in the colder weather.

When a snail comes out of hibernation, it pushes its epiphragm away and starts to crawl out.

Snails can survive in their shells all winter because their bodies slow down—which must be pretty slow for a snail! Hibernating snails do not eat. Their breathing and heart rate slow down. They don't use much energy at all. They can stay alive in their shells while the snow falls and the winter winds blow.

Snails stay tucked away in their shells during the winter.

Dry Spell

Sometimes snails will withdraw into their shells in the summer too. They will seal themselves in their shells if they are in danger of drying out during a drought. They make a mucus door and slow their bodies down to survive a dry season just as they do to hibernate in the winter. This kind of summertime hibernation is called estivation. A snail's shell and its mucus can come in handy any time of year!

Hibernation happens in the winter. Estivation happens in the summer.

Compare It!

The common poorwill is the first bird known to hibernate in response to cool weather. Its body temperature drops. Its breathing slows down. Its heart beats more slowly. The poorwill goes into a sleep state that might last for a few hours on cold nights. It can also last for several days or even weeks, depending on the weather. Like snails, poorwills can also enter this energy-saving sleep state during very hot weather.

Hopi Indians knew about the poorwill's hibernation long before scientists first discovered it in the 1940s. The Hopi call this bird the sleeping one.

Chapter 4

SLEEPING SNAKES

Garter snakes are found almost everywhere in North America. These snakes come in many different colors. Most of them are striped. They can live in a wide variety of places. The snakes can be found in forests, fields, and backyards. They can live from Mexico to Canada. Garter snakes can survive in all kinds of places as long as they can find water nearby.

Snakes slither outdoors during the summer. What do they do when it gets cold during the winter?

Some garter snakes are hibernators. Those that live where it's warm do not need to hibernate. But other garter snakes live where it gets very cold in the winter. These garter snakes have to hibernate to keep from freezing. And when garter snakes hibernate, they hibernate together.

GARTER SNAKES START GETTING READY TO HIBERNATE IN THE FALL.

Crowded during the Cold

Garter snakes hibernate in dens. A garter snake den can be any space that will keep the snakes warm enough when it is cold outside. Garter snakes might hibernate in the spaces between or under rocks. Tree stumps and old logs also make good winter dens for garter snakes. Garter snakes are known to go back to the same hibernation den winter after winter. They will even travel from far away to return to their winter dens.

A garter snake den can get pretty crowded.

Garter snakes hibernate in groups. There can be hundreds of garter snakes in a single den. There can even be thousands of snakes in a den. The Narcisse Wildlife Management Area in Canada has underground caves where tens of thousands of garter snakes come to hibernate. Every year, snakes return to these cave dens in the fall to hibernate. Garter snakes hibernate in groups to stay warm. They can keep their bodies warm enough to survive the winter by coiling up tightly against other snakes.

The Narcisse Snake Pits are in Manitoba, Canada. They are a popular place to visit.

Compare It!

Honeybees do not hibernate. But just like garter snakes, they survive the winter by spending it together. Honeybees huddle together in a winter cluster in the center of the hive. The queen bee is in the middle. The worker bees gather all around her. Then the worker bees begin to vibrate. The movement keeps the hive warm enough to protect the queen. The bees on the outside of the huddle keep changing places with the bees on the inside. This helps the worker bees stay warm too.

Bees use the honey in their hive for food during the winter. They will not survive if they do not have enough honey stored in the hive when cold weather comes.

From Den to Nursery

When spring comes, garter snakes are one of the first snakes to come out of hibernation. The male snakes usually wake up first. They leave the den and wait outside. Then the females wake up and leave the den. That's when the garter snakes mate. This gives the females enough time during the spring and summer to grow and give birth to their young before fall comes again. Hibernating together helps these snakes make the best use of each season all year long.

A baby snake is called a snakelet, a neonate, or a hatchling snake.

Chapter 5

TIRED TURTLES

When box turtles hibernate, they get even slower than usual! Turtles get their body heat from the air around them. When the air cools, a box turtle's body temperature goes down. Its heart rate and breathing gets slower. The plants and insects that turtles eat are hard to find in cold weather. Hibernation allows box turtles to survive the winter.

A turtle carries its home on its back. Why does it need to hibernate?

A Dangerous Sleep

Like other hibernators, box turtles do not eat while they are hibernating. They go without food for a long time. So they need to save energy. Slowing their bodies down helps them do this. But hibernating can be dangerous for box turtles. In fact, they can die from it.

TURTLES HIDE IN THEIR
SHELLS DURING HIBERNATION.

Eating Out

The length of a box turtle's hibernation depends on where it lives. Box turtles usually begin to get ready to hibernate in the fall. It takes a lot of energy to find, eat, and digest food. So a turtle starts saving energy by eating less and less food until its stomach is empty. The turtle then digs down into the dirt when it is ready to hibernate.

Turtles will usually stay asleep underground for three or four months.

Stranger Danger and Other Threats

Hibernation is dangerous for box turtles. They have to put on enough weight before it gets too cold. If they don't eat enough before hibernation, they won't have enough to live on during the winter. Box turtles don't move during hibernation either. Other animals can find them and eat them before spring comes.

If a turtle comes out of the ground too soon in the spring, the air might not be warm enough to heat the turtle's body. The turtle could die.

Location, Location, Location

Box turtles have to find just the right spot for hibernation. If their hibernation hole floods in spring rains, the turtle will drown. But the spot can't be too dry either. A turtle that gets too dry can get sick or even die. If a turtle doesn't dig deep enough to hibernate, it can freeze to death during the winter.

Young box turtles often die during their first winter. It is very hard for these turtles to survive hibernation. But they would not survive without it either.

Young box turtles might not make it through their first winter.

Compare It!

Alpine marmots also burrow into the ground to hibernate. They dig a hole and line it with dried plants. Then several marmots spend the winter together in the underground burrow. Being underground keeps the marmots warmer. So does being together in a group. Both of these behaviors help alpine marmots conserve energy. Sometimes young marmots have not stored enough fat to live on during the winter. They starve to death before spring comes. Hibernation is dangerous for young marmots just as it is for young box turtles.

Marmots are large ground squirrels. They are related to the prairie dog family.

Sleep On It

Hibernation helps animals survive threatening conditions. Scientists study hibernators to learn how to protect these animals. Studying hibernators might also help humans. Scientists believe that learning how hibernation works might be useful for people in many ways. It could help doctors learn how to safely freeze and thaw organs. That would make it easier to transplant them. Learning how to hibernate might even help humans survive travel to faraway planets someday. Scientists are discovering more and more about the benefits of sleep. We can learn a lot from the animals around us!

This scientist is weighing a hibernating hedgehog.

Extinct Animal Superpowers

- Cave bears were huge mammals that lived in Europe during the Ice Age. Skeletons of these bears show that they were twice as big as the largest bears alive today. These plant-eating bears had to hibernate in caves to survive the coldest weather, when there would have been no plants for them to eat.

- Being able to hibernate might be a superpower that protects animals from becoming extinct. Scientists think that being able to sleep through climate changes and times of food shortages might help animals survive extinction.

- As winters are becoming shorter and less cold, animals that once survived by hibernating through the winter are having their sleep patterns disrupted. They are waking up too soon or not going to sleep at all.

Glossary

behavior: a certain way of acting in response to a situation

burrow: a tunnel or hole in the ground made by an animal. *Burrow* also means "to dig a tunnel or hole in the ground."

conserve: to save something from being lost

develop: to make more available or usable

habitat: where an animal lives

mucus: a slimy bodily fluid that coats and protects sensitive areas

nocturnal: active at night

primate: any member of the group of intelligent mammals that includes humans, apes, and monkeys

restore: to put or bring back into existence or use

Learn More about Hibernators

Books

Glaser, Linda. *Not a Buzz to Be Found: Insects in Winter.* Minneapolis: Millbrook Press, 2012. *Buzz! Zip! Zoom!* When the weather is warm, insects are everywhere. But what do they do in winter? This book shows what twelve different insects do to survive the winter's chill.

Gray, Susan H. *Bears Hibernate.* Ann Arbor, MI: Cherry Lake, 2015. This book answers some of the most interesting questions about why bears sleep all winter.

Hirsch, Rebecca E. *Grizzly Bears: Huge Hibernating Mammals.* Minneapolis: Lerner Publications, 2015. Discover how and why grizzly bears hibernate.

Websites

Earth Rangers: Top Ten Coolest Hibernating Animals
http://www.earthrangers.com/wildwire/top-10/top-ten-hibernating-animals
Learn about some of the most interesting animal hibernators with colorful pictures and fascinating facts.

Frogs Are Green: Winter Is Coming—How Do Frogs Avoid Freezing?
http://frogsaregreen.org/winter-is-coming-how-do-frogs-avoid-freezing
Watch a frozen wood frog thaw out in the spring, and read more about the interesting ways different kinds of frogs survive the winter weather.

Ranger Rick: Wake Up!
https://www.nwf.org/Kids/Ranger-Rick/Animals/Mixture-of-Species/Wake-Up.aspx
Visit this website to find out how hibernating animals wake up when spring comes.

Index

Photo Acknowledgments

The images in this book are used with the permission of: © kolvenbach/Alamy, p. 4; © iStockphoto.com/MarkMirror, p. 5; J.M. Storey, Carleton University, pp. 6, 8; © Ingo Arndt/Minden Pictures, pp. 7, 12; © Hugh Lansdown/Minden Pictures, p. 9; © Smellme/Dreamstime.com, p. 10; © David Haring/DUPC/Oxford Scientific/Getty Images, p. 11; © Joel Sartore/National Geographic/Getty Images, p. 13; © Layer, Werner/Animals Animals, p. 14; © Isselee/Dreamstime.com, p. 15; © iStockphoto.com/Sasa Nikolic, p. 16; © Gary K. Smith/Minden Pictures, p. 17; © ANT Photo Library/Science Source, p. 18; © Laura Westlund/Independent Picture Service, p. 19; © Juniors Bildarchiv/F300/Alamy, p. 20; © LaineN/Shutterstock.com, p. 21; © David Shale/Minden Pictures, p. 22; © Rolf Nussbaumer/Minden Pictures, p. 23; © Sebastian Kennerknecht/Minden Pictures, p. 24; © Peter Darcy/Shutterstock.com, p. 25; © Mike Rogal/Shutterstock.com, p. 26; © Nigel Marven/Minden Pictures, p. 27; © iStockphoto.com/elleon, p. 28; © Dennis, David M./Animals Animals, p. 29; © iStockphoto.com/kathyclark777, p. 30; © Kent, Breck P./Animals Animals, p. 31; © Alessandro Mancini/Alamy, p. 32; © Chas. & Elizabeth Schwartz Trust/Animals Animals, p. 33; © Dr. Carleton Ray/Science Source, p. 34; © Misja Smits/Minden Pictures, p. 35; © Ed Simons/Alamy, p. 36.

Front cover: © Ted Kinsman/Science Source.

Main body text set in Adrianna Regular 14/20.
Typeface provided by Chank.